Two Thousand Years Too Late?

A Christmas Play by JOHN DEMPSTER.

COPYRIGHT

We do not ask for any "performing rights" royalties, but remind you that it is illegal to reproduce in print, by typing, writing or photo-copying, any part of this play without the Publisher's written permission.

No permission is needed, however, to perform this play, providing that copyright obligations, as listed above, are fulfilled.

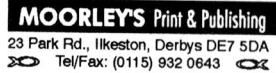

23 Park Rd., Ilkeston, Derbys DE7 5DA
Tel/Fax: (0115) 932 0643

ISBN 0 901495 63 8

CHARACTERS

The Producer — (Preferably a teacher: bossy and excitable, but capable of real sympathy)

Mary)
Joseph) — older, maturer children.

3 Shepherds)
3 Wise Men) — (In each of these groups, the 1st is older, and more questioning, the 3rd much younger, and a dreamer, and the 2nd somewhere in between)

TWO THOUSAND YEARS TOO LATE?

(<u>The only prop is, centre stage, a crib. It is empty. The characters are not costumed, for the play is a play about an 'undress' rehearsal.</u>)

PRODUCER : (Walks on stage, looking behind her. She is distinctly ruffled. In her hand she carries a script. Indeed, all the characters can have scripts, thus doing away with the necessity for too much learning) Look, are you pair coming ? We haven't got all night, you know. I want to get started.

MARY : (Off) Coming ! (She enters) Joseph's coming too. But he's just had an argument with the minister, 'cause his beard tickles.

PRODUCER : Well, he won't need to wear his beard tonight ! (Screams) Joseph !!

JOSEPH : (Hurries on) Sorry, sorry. A minor alteration ....

PRODUCER : Wow !

MARY : (Looking at the crib) But where's David?

JOSEPH : David ?

MARY : The baby ! David.

PRODUCER : He's not there.

MARY : I can see that ! But where is he? We can't have a proper rehearsal without him.

PRODUCER : Well, you'll just need to pretend he's there. (Pause) Oh, he doesn't need

                    to be there anyway. He hasn't a thing
                    to say. He's just......... there. No,
                    he's got teething trouble, and his
                    mum wouldn't let him out tonight.
                    Hopefully he'll be ready for our dress
                    rehearsal tomorrow night. Otherwise,
                    we'll need to borrow Lillibet........

MARY   :   You're not borrowing my doll.   I
                    positively refuse to allow it !

PRODUCER   :   All right, all right. We'll fight that
                    one out when we come to it. But let's
                    get started.

JOSEPH   :   I'm fed up already.

1ST
SHEPHERD   :   (Off) So am I. I think it's a stupid
                    idea pretending to be a shepherd.

3RD
SHEPHERD   :   (Off) Oh, don't be silly. It's fun !
                    I'd like to be a real ....

PRODUCER   :   (to Mary and Joseph) Right ! Stand
                    the way I told you. (They shuffle
                    about) That's right..... on on either
                    side of the crib. (They stand as
                    directed) No. Mary. Fold your hands.
                    In your lap ! Tha-a-t's right. And look
                    down. At your .... No !! Not that
                    far down..... yes, that's right.
                    (Pause) Now, hold it there.

JOSEPH   :   I feel daft !

MARY   :   (sweetly) You look it too.

PRODUCER   :   Never mind. It's only for ten minutes.
                    Oh ! Shepherds. Where are they ?
                    (She fumbles around with the script, and

then, in exasperation) Oh, I heard the silly clunks a minute ago! (Screams) Shepherds!

(<u>The three shepherds enter in a line, the smallest first, their heads bent. They kneel forming one wing of the 'V' with the crib at its apex. They don't notice that the crib's empty.</u>)

1ST SHEPHERD : (to Joseph) If you think your beard's bad, you should feel mine. It's <u>ten</u> times worse............

PRODUCER : Oh be <u>quiet</u>. Be like that third shepherd. He looks as though he's <u>enjoying</u> being a shepherd. (Pause) Now, back a bit! That's right! Now, let's <u>hear</u> you. We want your voice to <u>carry</u> ....

1ST SHEPHERD : (drones) We were out on the hills.

PRODUCER : Oh, sound as though you really were a shepherd.

1ST SHEPHERD : But I'm not!

PRODUCER : That's beside the point. Now, get cracking.

1ST SHEPHERD : (grimaces, then does his best) We were out on the hills ....

2ND SHEPHERD : .... watching the sheep in the cool, still evening.

3RD SHEPHERD : And Bethlehem rose on the hills behind us, flooded with light.

2ND
SHEPHERD : And high in the blackness above, the stars danced.

1ST
SHEPHERD : And then, suddenly, the sky was dark no more, but filled with light and sound and angel song.

2ND
SHEPHERD : And an angel cried out at us ....

3RD
SHEPHERD : And we were terrified. We started to run away, but the angel called out and said, "Don't be afraid. For I am here with good news for you, which will bring great joy to all the people. This very night in David's town your Saviour was born - Christ the Lord !"

1ST
SHEPHERD : And then the sky was filled with music. "Glory to God in highest heaven", the angels sang as loud as they could......

(Pause)

2ND
SHEPHERD : (His turn to speak, but he interrupts) Here, what does 'Saviour' mean ?

1ST
SHEPHERD : Oh shut up and let's get this finished!

3RD
SHEPHERD : That's not what you're supposed to say. You're supposed to say ....

PRODUCER : Excuse me! I'm the prompter here. Shepherd, you're supposed to say........

2ND
SHEPHERD : Well, I want to stop being a shepherd for
a minute, seeing that shepherds don't seem
to be allowed to ask questions, and I want
to know what a Saviour is.

3RD
SHEPHERD : Oh, hurry up and be a shepherd again
quickly. This is fun !

2ND
SHEPHERD : But what's a Saviour ?

MARY : A Saviour's someone who saves.

PRODUCER : So there you are, and now could we
please get going ?

2ND
SHEPHERD : But I don't understand..........

JOSEPH : (With superior patience) Well, if
you go swimming at the seaside in summer,
and the tide's going out, and there
are all sorts of currents and things,
you might find yourself getting dragged
out to sea..........

2ND
SHEPHERD : (dignity hurt) I can swim !

JOSEPH : But the sea's stronger than even the
strongest swimmer. (He hastily rewords
it, seeing the shepherd glowering)
Some-times. And there you are, getting
dragged further and further out to sea.
And what needs to happen ?

1ST
SHEPHERD : (impatiently) He needs to be rescued.

JOSEPH : (a regular Sunday School attender) He
needs someone to save him. And Jesus
was born to save the people on earth,
and that's why the angels were happy.....

1ST
SHEPHERD : But they weren't drowning. That was Noah.

MARY : Oh, do you always go to sleep at Sunday School? Of course they weren't drowning, but they wanted to get to heaven. You'd know if you listened! And they couldn't get to heaven no matter how hard they struggled, and so........

JOSEPH : They needed to be saved.

MARY : And Jesus is a Saviour. He was born to save people. That's what the angel told you.....

1ST
SHEPHERD : (startled) I never saw no angel........

MARY : No, I mean he told the shepherd you were pretending to be, that Jesus came to save.

3RD
SHEPHERD : (captivated by the crib, not realising it's empty) But how could a little thing like that save people ?

PRODUCER : Jesus grew up, and went about preaching and doing good, and in the end he was killed. He died. And that's how he can save us.

1ST
SHEPHERD : How ?

PRODUCER : Because he died ! I told you that !

2ND
SHEPHERD : Well, if I was to drop dead right now....

PRODUCER : Well ?

2ND
SHEPHERD : Well, I'd be dead, wouldn't I? And _I_ wouldn't _save_ anyone.

PRODUCER : Does _no_-one listen to the minister in this church? Jesus was able to save people because he was God's son..... he wasn't just an ordinary man. And it's because he was God's son that all the Shepherds and Wise men and people came to worship him after be was born in Bethlehem. Which is what our play's supposed to be all about if only we could get on with it. (Briskly) Now, all of you shepherds, get back into your line again. Oh no, not like _that_ ! Like _that_ ! Yes, just like you were before. Now, let's go right back to the beginning, and no interruptions this time _please_!

1ST
SHEPHERD : Oh, why do I _have_ to be a shepherd again?

PRODUCER : Well, you said you would be, and you can't drop out now. So get going !

1ST
SHEPHERD : Oh, very well ! (Pause: then, ferociously) We were out on the hills ....

2ND
SHEPHERD : .... watching our sheep in the cool, still evening ....

(_The 3rd Shepherd_, the youngest and smallest, a dreamer, has been staring fixedly at the crib. He has lost his concentration on what's been going on, and, in the middle of the _2nd Shepherd's_ speech, he interrupts)

3RD
SHEPHERD : (Hisses) Hey........ (Pause: everyone gapes at him) He's........ (He whispers, pointing) He's......... not........ there.

(Silence)

1ST
SHEPHERD : Whose not there ?

3RD
SHEPHERD : Jesus. (Softly) Jesus. The baby. He's <u>not there</u> !

PRODUCER : Of course he's not there. David's teething this evening, and his mum wouldn't let him come out.

3RD
SHEPHERD : (petulantly) Well, what's the use of coming to see a baby who isn't there ?

1ST
SHEPHERD : Oh, why worry? We're just pretending to be shepherds. And you're a lot better at pretending than I am. And it couldn't possibly be Jesus even if we had a baby.

Jesus hasn't been a baby for two thousand years. It'd just be David, pretending to be Jesus.

3RD
SHEPHERD : Oh, I don't know what you're getting at. I just want to pretend to be a shepherd...... a <u>real</u> shepherd. (eyes light up) And I wish you would too.

2ND
SHEPHERD : Let's pretend !

1ST
SHEPHERD : It's O.K. for you ! You could pretend you were a currant bun! You've got <u>imagination</u>.

Your teacher says that. But I can't pretend. I'm fed up being a shepherd.

2ND SHEPHERD : Oh come <u>on</u> !! Let's <u>try</u> ....

3RD SHEPHERD : But there's still no baby. And we need a <u>real</u> baby. We can't be real shepherds if there isn't a real Jesus for us to come and see.

1ST SHEPHERD : (The down-to-earth in him triumphing) Of course there's no baby ! We're too late. Years too late.

JOSEPH : Two thousand years too late.

1ST SHEPHERD : For Jesus the baby grew up into Jesus the man, and then at Easter time one year they took him and killed him, and now he's a Saviour, just like the angels promised.

MARY : But you've got to try to pretend. It's not hard, you know.......

PRODUCER : Of course it's not hard. That bunch are just being downright awkward. And as far as I'm concerned, they've <u>had</u> it. If they forget their lines tomorrow night, they can't blame <u>me</u>. I gave them a chance, and they wouldn't take it. And now it's the Wise Men's turn.

(Pause: then she screams) Wise Men !!

<u>(The Three Wise Men enter, and group to form the other arm of the 'V')</u>

PRODUCER : In a straight line, <u>please</u> ! No, don't <u>shuffle</u>. That's better. Now, kneel down. (They kneel) Right. You're the Wise Men. And you've got to pretend you really are the Wise Men, otherwise you'll be no good in the play at all. In fact, you'll be just as bad as that shower of shepherds over there. Silly boys ! Can't pretend for peanuts ! So <u>pretend</u> hard !

1ST
WISE MAN : We have travelled a long way.

2ND
WISE MAN : Many miles have we travelled across the hot desert, following ....

3RD
WISE MAN : .... a star in the sky for a guide. We saw it, and studied it, and knew from our books that it.........

1ST
WISE MAN : .... was no ordinary star, but a star to mark the birth of a great king.

2ND
WISE MAN : And so we followed it night and day, until it came here, and hung in the sky right above this place.

3RD
WISE MAN : So here we came too, to worship the great king sent by God. And we brought gifts.....

1ST
WISE MAN : I have brought gold. Rich, shining gold. Gold for the heavenly king..... (and he stretches out his hand)

- 12 -

2ND
WISE MAN : And I have brought frankincense. Sweet frankincense. Frankincense for the Son of God.... (he, too, stretches out his hand)

1ST
SHEPHERD : (cynically) All your pretending's a waste of time, you know !

PRODUCER : That's downright ir-ir-irreverent. You shouldn't <u>say</u> things like that about a Bible story.

1ST
SHEPHERD : But they're not real wise men. There were real wise men, two thousand years ago. But not them. They're just <u>pretending</u>.

2ND
SHEPHERD : They're doing it a lot better than you are.

1ST
SHEPHERD : But what's the <u>use</u> of pretending, when Jesus is a Saviour now, in heaven.

3RD
SHEPHERD : (<u>To Wise men</u>) He's not <u>there</u> ! (pointing) There's no-one to bring your gifts to.

1ST WISE
MAN : There's the baby.

3RD
WISE MAN : Is there ?

1ST WISE MAN : Well, it's only David, really. We just pretend he's Jesus, just like we pretend we're the wise men. And so we can bring gifts to the baby. Don't be a <u>dope</u> !

3RD WISE MAN : (he looks in the crib) But David's not in the crib.

1ST WISE MAN : Well pretend he is !!

(Pause)

JOSEPH : Look, we're getting hopelessly muddled up. We're pretending to be people for a Bible story. That's all. And we can go on pretending even if the baby's missing.

1ST SHEPHERD : Why should we bother? Just 'cause the minister wants us to ? And why shepherds, anyway? Shepherds are so <u>ordinary</u>.

MARY : But they were very special shepherds, because they came to Jesus when he's just been born.

1ST SHEPHERD : But that's past and gone ! Jesus hasn't been a baby for hundreds of years, and still we have to pretend he's still a baby?

2ND SHEPHERD : Oh, it's not that at all.........

1ST SHEPHERD : Yes it is. And he's not a baby. Because he grew up, and was killed. He died, and came back to life again and now he's a <u>Saviour</u>. And we don't <u>need</u> to dress up like shepherds to come and <u>visit</u> him. Because we can pray to him, and ask him to forgive us. He's alive! We don't need to pretend before we can come to see him.

(Pause)

JOSEPH : Alive ? Yes that's what we're told at Sunday School.

MARY : He's <u>alive</u>, and he can do everything you say he can.

JOSEPH : You're right ! We can <u>all</u> pray to him.

MARY : We don't need to pretend to be shepherds at all.

JOSEPH : And we <u>can</u> bring him gifts.

MARY : Not gold, like the wise men brought, for.....

JOSEPH : .... what use has Jesus with gold now, for ....

MARY : .... He's in heaven !

JOSEPH : But he wants us to give over our lives to him.

MARY : And live out our lives the way he wants us to

JOSEPH : And be <u>Christians</u>.

MARY : So we're <u>not</u> too late after all.

(Pause)

PRODUCER : Listen, please listen. It's true. But before it could be true, something had to happen.

1ST SHEPHERD : If he hadn't lived and grown up and died he wouldn't be a <u>Saviour</u> now !

PRODUCER : And before he grew up, he had to be <u>born</u>. And it's to remember that he was <u>born</u> that we're having our play. To remind people it's still not too late to meet Jesus, and that you believe he is a Saviour, by showing you believe he was born. And let's show we believe he was born by getting on with being Shepherds and Wise Men. Now. Right now. Please.

3RD SHEPHERD : I <u>want</u> to pretend anyway. I like pretending.

1ST SHEPHERD : Well, I'll pretend as hard as I can. If you really think it'll help people to know I believe it really happened.

PRODUCER : (her former self) I should think so too! Stand where you were before. No, <u>no</u>. ! A little to the left. A <u>straight</u> line. (Pause) Right ! Let's get cracking !

(They begin)

1ST SHEPHERD : We were out on the hills.......

2ND
SHEPHERD : .... watching our sheep in the cool, still evening.

3RD
SHEPHERD : And Bethlehem rose on the hills behind us, flooded with light.

2ND
SHEPHERD : And high in the blackness above, the stars danced.

1ST
SHEPHERD : And then, suddenly, the sky was dark no more, but filled with light and sound and angel song.

2ND
SHEPHERD : And an angel cried out at us..........

3RD
SHEPHERD : And we were terrified. We started to run away, but the angel called out, and said, 'Don't be afraid. For I am here with good news for you, which will bring great joy to all the people. This very night in David's town your Saviour was born - Christ the Lord !'

1ST
SHEPHERD : And then the sky was filled with music. 'Glory to God in highest heaven' the angels sang, as loud as they could.

2ND
SHEPHERD : And then they left, quick as they came, and all was dark and starry once more.

3RD
SHEPHERD : We thought it was all some strange dream.

1ST
SHEPHERD : But the angel had said 'Go see for yourself.
The baby you'll find in a stable........

2ND
SHEPHERD : ...... No room for him in the inn. The
baby you'll find in a stable......

3RD
SHEPHERD : .... And with it, its mother.

1ST
SHEPHERD : And with her, its father.

2ND
SHEPHERD : And so we came. To see. To believe.
To praise God for the Saviour he has
sent.

(Pause)

1ST
SHEPHERD : (faltering) And though I'm not really
a shepherd, and I don't like pretending
very much, I believe he was born, and
wish I'd really been one of the shepherds.
But I know he's alive right now, two
thousand years later, and that I can be his
friend. I want the church to know it
really was a Saviour who was born that
day, and so I'm pretending hard, to show
you how he was born.

MARY : I'm glad you came, Shepherds.

JOSEPH : The angel spoke to Mary too, you know.

MARY : Months ago, an angel came and told me the child would be born and told me the name to call him by, the name of the Saviour, the Son of God.

1ST
WISE MAN : We have travelled a long way.

2ND
WISE MAN : Many miles have we travelled across the hot desert, following ....

3RD
WISE MAN : a star in the sky for a guide. We saw it, and studied it, and knew from our books that it..........

1ST
WISE MAN : .... was no ordinary star, but a star to mark the birth of a great king.

2ND
WISE MAN : And so we followed it night and day, until it came here, and hung in the sky right above the place.

3RD
WISE MAN : So here we came too, to worship the great king sent by God. And we brought gifts......

1ST
WISE MAN : I have brought gold. Rich, shining gold. Gold for the heavenly king........ (and he stretches out his hand)

2ND
WISE MAN : And I have brought frankincense. Sweet
frankincense. Frankincense for the Son of
God...... (he too, stretches out his hand)

3RD
WISE MAN : (hands stretched out) And I have brought
myrrh. Bitter myrrh. Myrrh for the Son
who will die to save.

(Pause)

1ST
WISE MAN : O.K., I admit it. I don't like pretending
either. I'm not really a wise man. But
I believe Jesus is alive right now, and
wants us to give ourselves to him as gifts,
and follow him. And so, to show you that
I believe it's true, and that he was born
that day, I'm pretending I _am_ a wise man,
bringing my gift of gold.

MARY : I'm glad you came, wise men.

JOSEPH : Thanks for the gifts you bring.

MARY : And thanks for the love with which you come
to worship Jesus, the new born king.

(Profound silence)

3RD
SHEPHERD : Nearly as good as if the baby had been
there.

1ST
SHEPHERD : Just as good, for Jesus is in heaven now,
and we can pray to him all the time, and be
as close to him as the shepherds to the
crib.

PRODUCER : The hymn now. Softly please. (She speaks
           softly) Let's just sing the hymn.

    (And they sing)

" No room for the Baby at Bethlehem's inn,

'Sing to God' (Scripture Union) No. 48

MOORLEY'S are growing Publishers, adding several new titles to our list each year. We also undertake private publications and commissioned works.

Our range of publications includes: **Books of Verse**
Devotional Poetry
Recitations
Drama
Bible Plays
Sketches
Nativity Plays
Passiontide Plays
Easter Plays
Demonstrations
Resource Books
Assembly Material
Songs & Musicals
Children's Addresses
Prayers & Graces
Daily Readings
Books for Speakers
Activity Books
Quizzes
Puzzles
Painting Books
Daily Readings
Church Stationery
Notice Books
Cradle Rolls
Hymn Board Numbers

Please send a S.A.E. (approx 9" x 6") for the current catalogue or consult your local Christian Bookshop who should stock or be able to order our titles.